THE WIND, THE SEA AND I

THE WIND, THE SEA AND I

Kent Ramsing

Sunstone Press
Santa Fe, New Mexico

Photographs facing pages 15, 17, 30, 71, 126
by Louise Swenson

Photographs facing pages 19, 21, 23, 25, 100 and on pages 26-27
by Elizabeth Kuhner

Copyright © 1987 by Annette R. Ramsing
All Rights Reserved.
No part of this book may be reproduced in any form or by any electronic or mechanical means including information storage and retrieval systems, without permission in writing from the publisher, except by a reviewer who may quote brief passages in a review.

First Edition

Printed in the United States of America

Library of Congress Cataloging in Publication Data:

Ramsing, Kent, 1952-1977.
    The wind, the sea, and I.

    Poems.
    I. Title.
PS3568.A473W5   1987   811'.54   87-10212
ISBN: 0-86534-112-5

Published in 1987 by SUNSTONE PRESS
                Post Office Box 2321
                Santa Fe, NM 87504-2321 / USA

DEDICATION

To my son, Byron, Jr. for retrieving Kent's diaries after an eight month's search. To my dear friend Barbara Benziger for her devotion to Kent and for the hours she spent sifting through Kent's writings.

To Warrington Gillet, Mimi Strong and Jeanne Toomey for their kindness and interest in effecting the realization of Kent's dream.

Thank you,
A. R. Ramsing

CONTENTS

Foreword / 11
Introduction / 13
"Let Us Blow Up The Madhouse" / 27

Riding the Wind

Riding the Wind / 31
Witching Time / 32
Letter to S_____ / 32
Tell Me / 33
So Alone / 34
In Answer To Your Letter / 35
Waiting / 36
Fever and Fire / 37
The Builder / 37
A Tiny Fire / 38
Little One / 38
O, My Love / 39
Letter / 41
Letter To Pump / 42
My Girl of Summer / 42
In My Kingdom / 43
Thank You / 44
Question / 45
Deja Vu / 46
Pulse of My Life / 47
Silent Rivers, Silent Days / 48
Letter to N_____ / 49
For N_____ / 59

Abaddon! / 50
Love's Bridges / 52
A Sad-Happy Fantasy Dream / 52
Being Apart (To D_____) / 53
Memory of Chilmark and a Girl / 53
Children of the Sea / 54
Affirmative? / 55
Dream Spell / 55
Vision / 56
Young Summer Rain / 59
Circe's Wine / 60
Summer Blues / 62
Remembering / 63
Gardens of Violence / 63
Of Songs Sung in the Rain / 66
The Joining / 67
Solitude / 67

On Streets of Shattered Glass

The paths traveled . . . / 71
A Pause / 72
Murder Mystery Dream / 72
On Streets of Shattered Glass / 73
Crystallized Night / 73
Prayer for Rescue / 74
Orange Fever / 76
Prayer for an Answer / 77
Flight / 77
One Nightmare's End / 78
Prayer's Peace / 78

Betrayal / 79
Freedom's Shout / 80
Erebus / 81
Ballad / 82
Empathy / 82
Lost and Found / 83
Prayer for Release / 83
Rainbow-Riding Fools / 84
Metamorphosis / 85
Lost and Found / 86
Ones You Drive Insane and
   Then Say You Have Healed Them! / 87
This Time / 88
Dandelion Wine / 89
False Dusk / 90
First Christmas Away From Home / 91
Tomorrow / 91
Stream of Consciousness / 92
Dress Rehearsal Rag: A Ballad / 94
Cheshire Cat / 96
Prayer / 96
Reaching Out / 97

Reflections

Reflections / 101
The Wall / 102
The Dark Ways of Instinct / 104
Magic / 105
Philosophy / 105
Resurrection / 105

Spring / 106
Thought / 106
Dream / 107
Lost Child / 108
Now / 108
Flee the Sorcery! / 109
Facing Darkness / 110
Dream Journey / 110
A Sad Utopia / 111
Retrospect / 112
Night / 113
Listen / 114
Searching / 114
I Have Said Nothing / 115
Listen, Good Fellow Cockrobin / 116
Freezing / 117
Thoughts / 117
I So Miss Nature's Beauties! / 118
Rain / 119
Autumn's End / 120
Ode To the Full Moon / 121
Dolphin / 122
The Sea Child / 122
The Man of War / 122
The Vision / 123
Reveries / 124
The Long Ride / 125
Advice / 126

FOREWORD

I have been asked why I have copied and recorded Kent's writings.

I have done so for two compelling reasons. First, because among his diaries I found a request, saying that if anything should happen to him, that his only desire was that his diaries and writings be edited and, if possible, published and the returns thereof be used in support of the Mental Patients Bill of Rights.

Secondly, as unfinished and unformed as Kent's writings are, I think they reveal the incredible sensitivity, vulnerability, suffering and unrealized keen intelligence so often hidden behind the artificial, protective, defiant façade of the emotionally and/or mentally ill young person.

Why do they hide? Because no one **really** listens. I hear Kent saying "But Mom, no one really listens!" I, like many of those psychiatrists and other professionals I met in this field, never "really listened" beyond those façades. I am gambling that perhaps if just one parent or professional reads a young boy's heart, they will "really listen" sometime in the future.

A.R. Ramsing

INTRODUCTION

Kent Ramsing 1952-1977

It is my belief that because they are part of the human condition, loneliness and the desire for freedom have a universal appeal.

Because Kent Ramsing spent his adolescent and growing years from the age of fifteen to twenty-four, at which tragically young age he died, in psychiatric hospitals — places where the feelings of loneliness and the desire for freedom are a constant indescribable yearning — his poetry has a particular poignancy and beauty.

The spirit cannot be made captive and this brilliant young man's spirit was indomitable. The "system" never quite defeated him. In a sense, he triumphed over the indignities, the restrictions, the subtle and not so subtle cruelties, the punitive attitudes, the lack of understanding, compassion, sensitivity, and, at times, intelligence.

Throughout all the years of anguish, he escaped, not only physically at times, but also into the realm of his beloved books, and we now know his journals and diaries — a stream of consciousness writing — free-flowing, unforced. One wonders if he ever looked back at anything he had written; had he done so, one might assume he would have made a few corrections. Helping a little to bring order to his writings, in which prose suddenly turns into poetry, without pause, has been like unwinding spun gold.

A young, gentle, unlived life — a life beginning like a bird winging its way sky-ward ending in a meadow where he lay down to sleep in a warm night beneath the stars (how he must have missed them) a night in which snow covered him as he slept. He died from exposure, while in a state of complete physical depletion. His last escape from his last hospital. He died free, and I think this is what he would have wanted. A young man who should have soared to heights unknown, but who, for far too long and far too often, had his wings clipped.

I believe that had this young man lived at another time, and been able to sail "before the mast," or pioneer the west, he would have found outlets for his tremendous sense of adventure, romance, curiosity about himself and all aspects of life. He could have fulfilled his longing to experience living to the fullest, and found more of himself. He could have explored and roamed the world, and remained free; or perhaps he should have been a knight of old, performing daring deeds for his lady love, or searching for the Holy Grail.

I am convinced that had they lived today, some of the greatest geniuses of the past would have been locked up. Thank God, they dared to be different, indeed eccentric.

When Kent went back to the last hospital, after spending Christmas at home, my son, who is young too, asked, "What kind of world are we living in, wherein there is no place for this beautiful human being except behind bars and locked doors?" A question that demands an answer.

How painful and heart rending those bars and locked doors were to Kent is evident in his poems and, of course, he rebelled.

"Who in the hell are these rainbow riding fools,
Who are so keen at pretending they have found
You, when they have not the slightest idea of
Where to look for any child of night belonging
To some lost tribe of love's imagination?
Which group of people are you expanding
With your hearts?
I can see just as plainly as you bloody fools
If not further, with my eyes closed.
Some prophets stand within the breaking of each heart.
It's not easy this hurt that is with me whenever
I try to love, try to understand.

My heart doesn't break any more
It just gets down on the ground after dancing
Madly in its freedom, and crawls to a

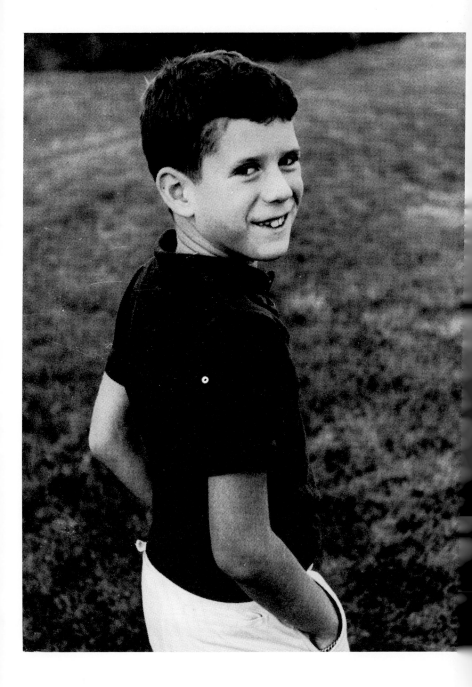

Hollow place in some fantasy forest and cries
Silently, yet loud enough for all the animals to hear.

I wish I could flow with the river and flow
Like quicksilver easily over each stone or
debris that blocks my way"

"But my prayers fly right and left and fall to shatter
in their brilliant
Colours, hastily scattering the birds,
then, I truly know I am alone." (written in isolation)

When Kent had had enough of the "white walls and corridors of lonely halls" he simply escaped. Time and again he escaped. He developed the fine art of escape to the point of becoming a legend. "One minute Kent was there, and the next he was gone." In lucid moments, almost anyone, including myself, has contemplated, from every angle, escaping from a psychiatric hospital. Very few have the courage and the imagination to carry through a successful plan. I am quite sure that most of the hospitals in which Kent was a patient were not accustomed to patients who perpetually tried to escape, and much less to those who frequently succeeded in so doing.

Kent's verse — "Let's blow up the Madhouse
     Let's do it today
     Let's blow up the Madhouse
     It's just in the way"
will warm many present and future patients' hearts, who long to escape physically as Kent did.

When his longing to roam the highways and byways became overpowering, he **was** on the open road, singing his songs of freedom in Colorado, Arizona, New Mexico, California, Montana, the East Coast from Florida to New England — he saw them all. How he managed to "liberate himself" so frequently will always remain a mystery both to his parents and the repeatedly confounded "authorities."

At one point during his peregrinations he lived with some

students, attending a university in New Jersey, as a sort of "bat boy," whose delightful presence was appreciated and enjoyed while he was present and missed when he felt he had to "turn himself in."

Sad to say, his illness and depressions caught up with him and he would usually be returned to the hospital. After one such episode he wrote:

"Slow down for awhile
for a good while
Until you find a place to smile —
(Hard faces are all around me
I guess I can't blame them for
hating me, I've been taking off
and hurting myself, and now I'm alone
and have to start all over again)
Oh well, I'm not going to fill their dreams
with cries and screams.
This time I'm going to make it."

How can a spirit like that be defeated? Or the rare courage of parents who allowed him to have these chances to be periodically free, because they knew it was the only way he could go on **living** in institutions, and not **dying**. This courage and unselfishness resulted in years of living through periods of agonizing fear, and almost unbearable anxiety, dreading the telephone ring, and yet longing to hear it, so that they would know where Kent was; searching for him when they didn't hear, and going from one end of the country to the other when they finally did hear from him or of him, to pick him up and take him back to the hospital. But he had his chances to experience the seas, the rain and all the other sights for which he yearned during his imprisonments.

Because their love for their son never wavered, because they never let him down, and were always supportive and never gave up hope, Kent's parents constantly remained about the only plus factor in his life. He was very much aware of this, and appreciated it, as he repeatedly told me.

The years of keeping up a "normal" life and cheerful front, bringing up their other children, unwilling to burden others with their devastating fears and heartaches, are indescribable, and difficult for others to understand who have not walked the same path.

It is a soul-searing experience for a family, and a shattering one, and when and if death comes, not only is there the emptiness of the loss of a beloved child, but the vacuum left that was filled for so many years with constant thoughts of this child and all the constant efforts made to improve his situation.

I first met Kent when he was a bright happy little boy of eight. When I saw him again, he had spent several years in psychiatric hospitals.

During the times Kent and I talked together, he told me that "they" (therapists, counselors, etc.) were continually telling him to "restructure his life." He said so pathetically, "How can I restructure my life when my life has never had a chance to attain any structure? I have nothing to relate to, to go back to. I have never had the opportunity to develop any true identity, or sense of self. How can I reconstruct that which never existed? I feel so sad and left out when I come home now. I have no friends my age left, with whom to pick up a relationship — they have all moved on — made lives for themselves, whereas I . . . "

Therefore, although he would eat his heart out in each hospital with his desperate longing to come home he would end by realizing that the only other young people of his age with whom he could identify were back in the dreaded and frightening hospital — and he knew he had to return.

So often suffering and anguish seem to us so meaningless, especially when we are haunted and taunted by the "might have been." Yet, in Kent's case, I think the legacy he left his parents, his family, and the countless tortured souls who are suffering and who will continue to suffer in the same ways he did, gives it all meaning. Because of the tragedy and

seeming waste of his youth and young manhood he will speak perhaps especially to the young who may share his same agony and in whose behalf he raises his voice in protest and in love. **All** those he reaches will be helped by this moving expression of his young life.

His parents' memories of him hurt deeply but they are beautiful ones and precious beyond compare. They are the ones that will last the longest.

A happy loving childhood. A handsome, lively, full of mischief, utterly captivating winsome little boy, with an enchanting smile, mercurial in his expressions, intensely sensitive, generous to a fault; curious about the world unfolding around him — nature, plants, trees, flowers, animals, fish, marine biology — devouring books on these subjects; dissecting a frog with a friend on the driveway of his house at night by flashlight. A child who sang solos in the church choir and school with the purity of voice only little boys have, and who, when his mother picked him up at school would say, "It's happy I am that the sunset is so beautiful." A child who, when his parents returned from a trip bringing presents for all their children said, "Thank you for just coming home." A little boy who, at the age of six, when fishing caught a many brightly hued dolphin, watched it die on a dock with its colors all faded, and went home to write a poem mourning this loss.

Once he said to me, "But they just can't seem to understand what I go through." They understood more than he ever knew, and I did tell him, "Kent, no one who hasn't **been** there can possibly totally understand the experience." This was our bond in common, although I knew I didn't suffer as much or for so long.

A quote from a typed sheet of paper he kept tacked to a bulletin board in his bedroom at home:

"With all its sham, drudgery, and broken dreams, it is still a beautiful world."[1]

Above all he, who was so tormented, wanted peace, inner peace. His favorite prayer was St. Francis of Assisi's:

"Lord, make me an instrument of thy peace."

In case of his death, and he seemed in his writings to have a premonition of early death (and a cold one), he gave his brother a tape asking that it be played at his burial — "Bird on a Wire." How well he knew himself in many ways. It is a tragic song, full of regrets and longings, ending:

"I have tried in my way to be free."[2]

I shall always think of Kent as searching. From a tape he had, come the verses put to a haunting melody:

> "I sit before my only candle
> Like a pilgrim beside the way
> I hold out my only candle
> With so little light to find my way."[3]

In Kent's last letter to me, a hopeful letter, he said, "I shall be so glad when this strange odyssey is over."

My hope and prayer is that the "odyssey" of this shining rebel against the circumstances in which life placed him, has just begun.

Barbara Field Benziger*

*Author:"The Prison of My Mind" (Walker and Company, New York); and "Speaking Out" (Walker and Company, New York)

1. "Desiderata" — Max Ehrmann
2. "Bird on a Wire" — Leonard Cohen
3. "Song For Adam" — Jackson Browne

Let's blow up the madhouse,
Let's do it today,
Let's blow up the madhouse,
It's just in the way

RIDING THE WIND

Riding the Wind

Summer like an eagle's cries
Vanishes and glides
On gray and silver clouds
    in our sighs, —
Oh! come back riding the wind
Come back I cry!
Gone like my dreams
Sea wind uttering
An exile far away
    from my simple home.

Far away on some secret isle
    in some simple paradise,
I take your voice melting in the city
Singing memories of our eyes.
Seeking moments of innocence
    shaping heartfelt truths
Ridding our love from empty lies,
Passing away, drifting seasons,
Resurrected from bloody shrouds.

    Ride the music, ride the wind
      to the sun!
    Ride the music here to my
      empty arms,
    Ride the wind!

Witching Time

Falling into the hot earth
As the green flies and turns
    Young bodies yearn
Jewel filled fire urns
Await us in the blue caves
The goddess of the lions
Waits in her virgin park
Protected by children of the dark
Come, with me my little one,
It's time we close our eyes to the light
And walk through the gentle forests of the night

Letter to S_____.

May you find time which will never stop
Unless, no one awakens to fill themselves
   with sun, wine and, strange, but joyful
   wisdom to linger and realize that you
    could only be known as love comes to know
   an eternal innocence as her brother.
Life can never enchain you,
   but will flow as in golden waves,
   or gems made in air around and around.
Laugh sometime for a friend
For your eyes mischievously become sunrise
   and your warmth condemns every
   narrow philosophy,
Which cannot in freedom's trials withstand.

Tell Me

As I rise up from this soft nether world
You, my friend, from a dream of a child's
    dimension
Tell me more of love crashing into oblivion
    Of the eagle's sky.
    And I wonder why
I left my powers of childhood behind?
A time to see with your soul
When one's eyes go blind.
    To say once more,
        Today,
    I love you
To think of how I felt when we first kissed!

So Alone

Dance, rejoice for a moment
   in your woods of freedom
Leaving me behind calling your name.
Seeking for some different game
   I would play,
Some enchantment to catch your grace
freeze your movements in a daze —
To turn your spirit towards me for the
   rest of my days.
   (But I remain chasing a nymph
     through the forest,
   Swimming with dolphins in the sea
     through oceans of love)

She pretends and will not take part in the dance
She, with her mind which destroys dreams
   And who runs from romance —
Playing free in her own world alone
She does not think of the desolation
The game she plays is her solution
Of the story. Her only consolation.

   (But my time in isolation
     And her kisses
  Have made me feel
     so all alone)

In Answer To Your Letter

Flying
   Silently, freely
Overhead gulls swirled
Over the ocean in the
Morning rain
And all around was a tide
     of heavy pain
     perhaps it's the
   Strangeness of time
     lost again —
Fare thee well
   fare thee well
     Remembrance
     Embraced in
       the summer rain.

Waiting

My love runs my life in her games
Though she doesn't realize
We're walking through clouds
My love lies deep in my heart
Alone, suffering winter behind this door,
My feelings well up from within me
As the ocean waves far away at home
Wash the dust away from the feet
Of my love's funeral shrouds.

We are walking by the railroad tracks,
Each waiting for the train
I wonder where it will stop
And who will be aboard?
As love takes me on another journey
To fulfill her needs.
For at the end of a rainbow
God would see that I had wings
To fly my love home.

I spend my night in lonely confusion
And love awakens me
To times of delusion
I almost desire to bring it to an end
But I cannot, for she is my friend.

Fever and Fire

I feel her warmth
Building fever pitch
As if brought about
By some magic I possess.

I feel her need
But respect her wish
As she heads for bed
In a green light alone

Returning to my room
I light a cigarette
And am followed by two aides
Who accuse me of arson!

The Builder

The ghosts of my fantasies
Surrounded me as I stood
Wondering like music in the warm.
I once knew strong life with you
A life renewed each day as we blessed
The sun god with our innocence in the sea
I shall build a sanctuary of peace for
    you with my tears.

A Tiny Fire

    She waits for someone
To rescue her from a type of pain
That's easy to understand
    But hard to explain
(All the young saints are into it)
    She came like cold rain
Into my life and I lit a tiny fire
    To keep her warm.

Little One

Born to innocent delight
Let her sleep into the
beginning of light
She will see the
Sacred place soon
the altar and the stone
in the full moon —

O, My Love

O my love
So near yet
so far away
Reading a book
the lines so
True to heart
for our losses
from a sad play.
Sometimes it's hard
to see the light
At the end of the night.
Seeing you standing
With some other's
heart in your
hand, at the end
of the tunnel,
Where the greener
grass spreads.
The old words
I need to speak
Siphoned, poured thru
a funnel
Just collect dust
in my head
And this need
for expiation
fills my empty soul
With a weighty dread.
The worlds change
like the Rhythms
of a solitary dance,
When I look upon
You, I fall into
a sad trance —

We had a lot
we had to learn
About each other,
but we never
took the chance
And now, I can't
Pretend to hide
in the garden
Someone must tend
Now I can no longer
conceal the heart
that I can't alone mend.
I remember the vow
the token, the promise
our bodies had spoken
tied and held together
with strands of
a spider's web
The lonely weaver
who broke the
silver thread shot
From our angels joining
our eyes,
melted now by tears
cut by lonely sighs
pulled into each
solitary corner
by fool pride's lies.

O my love let me turn
to a Paradise
of ocean and castles
in the skies.
You feed your mind
with a sad book
of how much

a devil took,
the swine that
ate the pearl.
How my candle is
kindled by
Just one look
at your eyes
Past which
My longing flies!
How can it be
that love kindled
by the sun
     dies?

Letter

When the bird flies out of range
   from the hunter's gun
We shall join together again
   and have our child-like fun —

My mind bled for us in the land
Of the lost and dead
As there was so much fear
    filling my head.

But today I fell from heaven
As I rolled out of bed
And awoke, strong and young
Purified from yesterday's purgatory.

  I can again look at you —
      and love! —

Letter To Pump

Dear Pump,
    I'm worried about you.
I'm getting better somehow, but I don't feel very strong. I guess I just take the light. I hope by the time you get this you're feeling better, since you're sick tonight, there's a storm — thunder and lightning.
    I have a little plant that I named after you. I don't know what kind it is, but you'd like it. Maybe, if it does well, you will too.
    Love,
        Kent

My Girl of Summer

I cry repentance to the Lord, Jesus,
    yet Judas, the priest
Shook himself in self-righteous wrath —
    and betrayed
    my girl of summer,
Who walked the Saviour path —
    Are we then saved?
        or
            forgiven?

In My Kingdom

Ruby red light
Sparkling like refracted
Time spread through
The castle windows
Graceful maiden hands
As white and gentle
As a dove,
Clasp my hands
Bejewelled with mystic rings
Bearing the symbol
Of my kingdom audaciously
Her face so full yet aquiline
Her eyes like green fire
Shine fiercely into mine
A lighter hue of blue
Against the new sky
In the new land
Where gentle people
Wander free!
I am the king
And you are my queen
During the reign —
    The moment of a gentle song.

Thank You

To _____,
    who,
Tiptoes in silence
around my bed
and quiets the raindrops
that fall upon my head
I'm glad you're here
to brush away my pain.

Your eyes laugh and search
Your sharp words lighten my
   sad heart.
My soul rises when you comfort
   my crazy head,
And I thank you for your care
   though brief —
I'm not alone, when you're there
I can't feel dead when I know
   you care.
   The sickness is a lot easier to carry
   and bear,
      thank you.

Question

Early morning fever runs through my sleepy
   veins from eight o'clock to noon,
I wander through a lazy nervous gloom
Can I take the weeks ahead in stride?
So she whom I love can look to me with pride?

Remembering as I rest, the many lovely
   rides of our passion
though that was summer and now as this
   winter holds no mystery,
I spend the early morning seeking her shelter
   in the future of spring,
From my hunger and misery I wait for our new
   love to blossom and again begin.

But now my head in a song swims around
   and around
My legs shake and I can't speak
   a sound!
Shall she hear my silence echo nothingness?
Or see my actions?
Read my feelings?
And hear soft longing sounds, as invisible blood
   drips from my tiny wounds?

Déjà Vu

I am going now into the Long tunnel
Take my reaching hand
Come and follow me
The end of death is
   near the light at the end
   seeming to be so far away —

Let us enter into this other Land
Of the forest so green
So innocent so nice
With the sun sifting through
   the morning mist

Look ahead not behind
The past now —
Would leave us blind
Now we are free
To follow this ancient road
There are many mysteries
     Still to be seen —

Pulse of My Life

In the sun
Resting
    feeling
the sweet rays
seep into me
Until I can no longer rest
My heart beating wildly
Within my young chest.

The erotic floats freely
released insistently
by my inherent longing for you
We swim in lakes
  and bask naked
In the soft evening light
Sleeping wrapped together
   in gardens of cool morning dew

We dance in time
  with flashing green
  and silver in an imagined night
Making love in the sand
by a golden sea
Or playing in warm summer rain
Like children so free —
And I remember the
Pulse of my life within you
With the whole of your soul
    surrounding me.

As I lie with sad melody
a sad song in my heart
I also remember the bird
in the cage of your breast

fluttering wildly against mine
The memory drugs me like some
   ancient wine.
And I feel the power
  the sweet magic of
  longing arise
I look into the sun
  in the clear summer skies
I wait for your touch
  and your kiss
Yet hide from your eyes.

Silent Rivers, Silent Days

Changing places, bodies grasped —
You change the part only of the time,
And the ghost has its revenge.
Silent rivers flow through my mind,
The thorns crown me, while I
Wander through the past. —
Clear light! clear light! I must take
And find the center before
I waste away in this strange, queer town!
I drift through silent days without you
Only the spirit's body,
Only the dark shadows visit me
With sorrow and unnoticed deaths. —
I feel the arrow in my dream
Only tell me, once again, of your
Lord and Saviour before I drift
    away! —

Letter To N_____

Dear N_____,

I knew tonight that you just said "goodby" to me when you said "See you someday."

All of us are searching, everyone is. I know your message is that I shouldn't look any further than myself, but, girl, I'm afraid! So I look further, I've lived searching and I've done a lot of fouled up things, things you wouldn't think me capable of!

I've lived like this for so long, that it is hard to see. People, no matter who, are also animals, and so I've lived in the Zoo. I can't stand anything about the way I've lived my life, but all I **know** is this. So it's easy to reach through windows and grab at new things.

Don't you think if someone said to me "Here is the starting line" I'd start? My whole problem is **where** to begin. N_____, even though in most ways you have more against you than I, you have purpose and direction. I don't.

I'm not writing this for sympathy, I just want you to know what I'm up against so you won't be hurt by my confusion. If you still want to call me, I do care for you, I do.

    Love

        Kent

For N_____

I'll never forget seeing
N_____ running wild against
   the sun
I hope she finds someone
   to love
It hurts me to see her trying
   so hard
Not to let me know how
   hurt she is —

Abaddon!*

I reach the angry denial, the petty death
the ghosts of you and her in every breath
I watch my silver† for fallen faces
And hear the gallows of your mind pull the traps
   for one more fallen angel to keep a
   sinner and a fool in wraps.
I see the bloody bed go flooding by
And my vein bursts open in the summer sigh.
Oh! sweet haunting melody to teach such fright
Where angels flee in a swooning day or night
And children pet the dogs that bite.
A light appears, expands in the gloom
   as your curious soul flies in the room
     to seek the murder, or your secret loom
     to hide inside, a dream of doom.
The hideous veil of symbolic look,
Into the realms arcane or story book
   the vagrant realms so fiction free
     of living demons haunting me
Cannot replace the soul you called and took,

Time is all, to be first or last
Hold fast before we lose our grasp
   on memories pure and good
   in shrouded sleep where if I could,
I would not drown forever in that dreadful sea
Where past and present all are one;
Peopled with vigilant deceivers and
   deeds of darkness long since done
where ghosts of friends in the setting sun
Point narrow fingers declaring me the one
   the voices die, the walls fall silent.
   Forgive me now of all things past,
Like a wounded soldier I lose my grasp,
       — and fall condemned —

* Abaddon — place of destruction, depths of Hell. Rev: 9:11
† old English for mirror

Love's Bridges

The only bridges love has are invisible
   the only change from reality
   is but an abstraction.
Why then do people spend a tired moment
   slicing their hearts because I own —
   you own — **they** own the wooden
   ridges of the African mountains?
My lady is lost and I miss the creation
   I've invented of her golden eyes!

A Sad-Happy Fantasy Dream

I have seen faces of pure mist
    within my dreams.
It is these people I am
They spoke to me of what they seek
Yet cannot find and sang songs
   of their love and pain.
I wandered in the spring and reached a plateau
    where the flowers bloomed
    like flowers on a tree —
I prayed in my sleep at your temple of jade
    but saw a panther in the woods
    which wandered gently and proudly
    through the emerald glade
   It was a carnival of chance
Which brought you to me again in my sleep
    We spoke to each other
      As if we'd never been away —

Being Apart (to D_____)

I feel your absence in me
Like a thread traversing a needle's eye
Everything I do,
or think
or feel
has its colors in it.

Memory of Chilmark and a Girl

During the short legend of darkness
I walk upon a stage of solitude
With no audience to behold.
Realizing I should be wandering
To a remembered transient home!

And shifting to love
Instead of watching
The black cruel tide wash and pull
My castles into time's invincible eye
Indigo sea of space!
Suffering like the first
   of the lost lovers
Searching through seas everywhere
   ageless through time —

Rebellious tragic young fools
Singing drunken songs
Writing down dreams
   or themes
Born from wine —
While her protector conjures
With heavy sighs

The young girl's eyes
Grow more lost and wild
Branches of a secret concern
Shoot from my being!

A gentle hand
I lay to rest
on your cheek
softly like the touch
   of a feather
As you turn startled
   from the lie of a song
Wondering like me
Where you belong —

Removing an intimacy swiftly
I start to speak of nothing —
And while the house slides
Off the cliff down into the sea
I search through photographs
An amateur artist left
   of you and me. —

Children of the Sea

I remember her well,
Besides being lovers,
We were children of the sea.
And we often caused each other
The joy and pain of the sea.

Affirmative?

The question one has to answer tonight
   is in the affirmative —
Shall I love the girl who haunts this dreary place
   of my life and death?
Or remain forsaken by the one who has cradled
   my heart, only to scorn it,
And leave me wandering the lonely forests and fields?
Shall I turn to her, disguised as she is,
A wood nymph for comfort, who immediately
Would yield to my desire —
Before my soul is set afire
As autumn's sacrifice?
What new feeling will come together
   What will suffice?
The question I have to answer should be
Answered in the affirmative
   but will she listen?

Dream Spell

She wanders through paisley gardens
   with her new love, she has no
   need for me,
   yet I feel her still near me
   and, in her heart,
She dreams the dream
Which holds me in its hand
   a spell without a fade.

Vision

It is the happenstance
   of the time
The bay seeming
   across to a new
   Bright land as it was
   and jewelled nature
   sparkled brightly
   and all too clearly
Reflected an image
   of a lovely day
The gold shone from
   the new city,
   the new Egypt, the
New Babylon as it
   could have been
   had it developed
   not from the life
   in which
      lacked something
   in which
   was so much.
Though it came
   suddenly from
   the ground
   it came not from
   the ethereal dirt.

I have crossed
   fields in my mind
   climbed mountains,
   lived in the sea.
I have made love
   in the sun
With those who

    assumed goddesses
  in a union of
  a clear sky,
And I have talked
  the talk of Olympian
Gods with my humble
  friendly peers.
Though I have seen
  the longing in your
  eyes, I felt it more
  in your open smile
For it remains
  through your ordeals
  the questioning smile
    of a child.
We will embark
From another flesh
And will begin a
Journey naked, an
Exploration into time.
We will clothe ourselves
  in our experiences
And, hopefully, arrive
  in front of love
  to accept it removed
  from all but what
  is held inside us
  that is good.
Will you come with me
Or shall it be a long time?
Some day we will reach our
  Destination together
  and praise God's
  heavenly soil and
  sing like the happy
  Ancient in the wind.

When I looked
   across the bay today
The sun shone down
Warmly on my memories
   of just a year's past
   and made the city
look newly arrived
as if set down by
   God's Hand
or is there a god
   of any sort
Except for Life?

Young Summer Rain

I am a writer
In the sun
A walker in warm rain
walking the rain-drenched
Streets,
Singing half a happy song.
Come join me under
The lamplight

At her gate
I stop and stare
   at rain pillaging
Warm summer air
We are old,
But a little young
She will join me
In tomorrow's sun.

Circe's Wine

Inside your spiritual
life is a part of me
That passed silently
Pervading my essence
life newly awakened
in our individual
concepts
      emotions
perceptions
Bore itself towards
simply something new
like the quiet aqua-green
waves in the summer
caressing the shore kindly.
  Rippling warm silver
  beads
      sparkle endlessly
      in the sun
  like children's laughter
  in young eyes alive
  shining
      dreaming
  always wondering
  what will become
  in the next minute
      next hour
the next sunset hanging over
the ocean typically red with
its glowing love, or mine with
Just a day, a person
      another person
and another
seeming a bright orange
center of the beginning

such a beautiful nucleus
of love, birth and youth!

Fixed with joyful
awe we should
stand and watch
   the seed of life
We should open our
souls together, friendly
   open our minds
As we evolve so rapidly
   from day to day.
I should by all standards
   say remain to chart your
lives by others and not withstanding
time, and not knowing of self
I should say remain
   but with such freedom
held happily within us
to burst forth unexpectedly
I cannot, for it is the beginning
of summer and summer is
like Circe's wine!

Summer Blues

Someday blues with
All your pain
Still falls within the sleepy rain
And all of everything
   fills your eyes with green
Walk and try to stand
It's all a mistake
With someone's lost hand
And I fill my head
      I cannot comprehend
  the days I've lost
  the years estranged
  the time tossed about on
  the sea
     can I grasp
  Just a young hand reaching? —

Someday blues with
All of everything
Withheld in the rain
travel down
      Sleep awhile —
I'll remember your smile
  on a summer day.

Remembering

Remembering sunlight and your
   warm wine laughter
I will cry because it's strange and lonely
   to be continually set back waiting —
   And I'll love you because I am still the stranger
   who will never leave you
   For I will dream of you
   As always being my friend.
But I shall no longer join this strange race
For I no longer have a death to face.

Gardens of Violence

To hear harsh bloodstained words from her sinks
knives in my heart
To know she sits
with him whom
I torture alone
in my dreams
tears my soul
apart and the
ancient blackness
rises from the
devil of my mind
and begins to flow
like syrupy poison
through my veins
until I can think
of nothing but
her and my love
that hangs on to
itself while hopes
crumble like lost

travellers on a
suicidal road

My love for her remains even through
the aura and veil
of Satan's hatred.
I still sense when
I hear her sweet voice
that she is
still my woman
Yet I long to run
from the gardens
of violence, death
and revenge that
exist within the
pain created by
my foolish acts.

I search for signs of peace
to interpret in
the symbols of
my dreams when
I awake in the sad
day, to find the raven
fly past my prison
window bearing the
blackness of my evil
almost proudly.
At times she is my child,
a demanding one,
and I am
an inadequate father.
Night falls as I return
to my books to seek
new worlds of magic
beyond these walls

God hears not my voice
And the demons of my
sub-created universe
confused my prayers.
O! I would forsake
King death at any cost
if I could but free my
soul once more and
soar above this time
to the rainbow kingdom
Where the queen of the angels
dwells and there I could
live among the priests of
the kingdom and consult
them to where I should go.

Yet I remain trapped
in a cage of visions
of doom, on lost highways
among treacherous friends
and I reign in the court
as king of my exile
as king of my last asylum
a prince waiting for his princess' return!
but as I wait I die
lying huddled against
the cold wall
in my best friend's
coat —

Of Songs Sung in the Rain

In the good days I would be a rambler
   with comrades roaming
through the strange lands of
   unconscious exploration —
We would speak with the spirits
   of our strange nights
And laugh in the time of our youth —
   I would leave,
Leave behind unsure loves
And new found friends, outside of various
   laws.
   With cords snapped
   I would be gone
Into lonely worlds of sad change
Watching for the dove to fly to my windowsill
   from the sunset
With some soft message
   of love for me —

Can you find my heart along the
   highways?
Of songs sung in the rain?
Can you see me wandering through my
   planes and spaces?
Falling, with disbelief, with the weight
   of things left undone,
To land lost in broken pieces, out of place
   in this world?

It's taken me time to blossom from red ground
   I await the tide to wash the castles
      of an old day away —
   I await the orgasmic release of seas
      crashing within me
         freed, at last —

Today in the withdrawal of hidden need,
My time of tears from love,
Longing to break from my heart.
My heart is spent in the spell of her eyes
Memories grow cold within the pit of my
    being.

The Joining

Hell ceases to be hell
    when you find love
And heaven and hell
Shall join in peace.

Solitude

These girls are pretty and nice but
  I want to be alone.

Carry me far away from
  the realm of this place
And into a paradise of love!
    Love, yes I know of love —
    It is a summer's passion
    and a dying flower —
    Faith is a tide of birds
    which soon fall to earth —
    Friendship is a ghost of revelry
    in an empty tavern —

      Give me the solace of solitude!
      Give me the liberty of space!
      And the gentleness of the summer
        rain —

ON STREETS OF SHATTERED GLASS

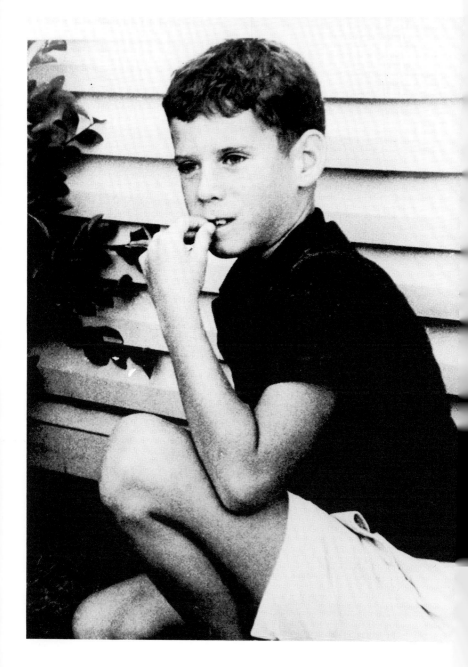

The paths traveled . . .

The paths traveled
Perhaps even the trials
  of my life —
lead me again to that
  clarity and that road
  I now follow
Hidden once by my clouds
  of fear and doubt —

The castles, where I went to hide,
The knowledge, learnt from many,
A sun flower, damp with morning dew.
The fawn, the innocent waves crashing
Gently against the soft white shore,
The sun rising anew, majestically
For those who have come here to
    wait
      and
        watch.

A Pause

Today my mind is silent
Burned clean by the furnace
   of my nightmares —
I flash the present and
The past falls to ashes
As I fly towards
The ocean of tomorrow —
The myths have lived within us
   for too long
Fantasy replaced by clarity
Normalcy to replace the bizarre

   It's time soon to begin
   And time to follow the seagulls
   Flight into the day
      into the tropical night —

Murder Mystery Dream

I pause to remember a murder mystery
   dream —
He was my other self and we were very
   good swimmers,
The phantom is my own thought form,
   an elemental force created by wanton
   thoughts and imprisoned days in exile.
He has much to tell me of my journey's
   end.
He should know many things,
He has watched closely.
He hasn't spoken or appeared this year.
I don't know what that means or the
   strange quiet of this time of day.

On Streets of Shattered Glass

On streets of shattered glass, I saw them run
  in fear, in time with one another,
  The noise of cluttered happenings past
  came screeching, burning to halt at my feet,
    My friends move much too quickly
    to a slow clock
    Hastening gestures, and quickened glances
      entice me to run with them, winning
      the race, left far behind,
    Their youth is only velocity
My flame shall not die at once, for I have lit my
  watch fires and seen my face in my own mirror.

Crystallized Night

What we do to life, our transient friend
Death does to us in the end.
Yet hate the shape, despise the ugly worms
Death follows life in many forms
Life's foolish laughter is a thorn in my ear
All my friends' efforts are born out of fear
As heros and athletes charge with amazons
Through hate-poisoned hours which feel like a year
A time with a bastard king, sitting with a
  company of thieves.
Life's bastard son in the asylum
  he grieves
As lizards and snakes of the religious mind
Crawl through his dreams
Life is just not what it seems
And I no longer travel or see
Through the nights so crystallized —
Death has snuck into my soul
  and sees through my eyes.

Prayer for Rescue

pain
    warped a time
within
    a live love
that smashed
its poor head
    against a prison
wall
    and died
    a fallen angel
me, in a sick
ungainly interlude
as i groped
and felt for my eyes
    recoiling
    inside
my heart writhes
as you see into the
rotting remains of
the pathetic
    and sickening
attempt
at a completely futile
    existence
cheapened consistently by
crime
    let us pray that this
    foolish creature
    will plague my soul, me, no more,
    the phantom double.
    O! sorrowful vengeance
    O! night of a succubus
    dwelling with prince madness

in my room, o terrible leopard
of my mind hast thou not had
enough innocent blood to
satisfy your savage desire?

   o! god, o! god i ask not
   but to live satan free
      of my heart!
   o! ocean receive me gently into thy arms
i stand at the cross with a willow branch
      and a knife
   synchronized in the presence
      of You
i walk at the edge of falling
        lord god catch me!

Orange Fever

Sunlight shining
   Through dreams
Of yesterdays rain
Burns softly into
My room with holy
Shafts to bless and
   Sanctify each corner
   Of my pain.
The cursèd locusts
   Feed upon
Ripples of thought
Within my tired brain
Fatigue from an unchartered
Source rests with my spirit's bed
with hollow voice
Yet plaintive cry
As I feel the hours
Of my soul slip by
Into dimensions soft, dark
   And perverse
     With the orange fever
     Of the split wound
     Which is my sickness
The dream of such a gentle soul
To strive and reach summer's goal
   of peace!
Tonight may I dream of her again.

Prayer for an Answer

I question a hundred gods when I arise
(dark Lord, dying in a humid gloom)
I'm answered by the voices of a thousand
   damnèd in gnashing sin
   oh glory to win?!
"As I lay me down to sleep
I pray the Lord my soul to keep"
   I beseech, I demand
     I rise, I fall,
       I understand —
The mystery with no answer.
Oh! Flee not! Heed my soul here!
   I know of no answer
   to that ultimate complaint
      Why?!!

Flight

Once I felt I was a bird
Deprived of the skies
   highways
Until the song told me of its
   pain,
As it still passes chanting a holy
   force
Still the wind was left in your
   eyes.
I was, I felt, only there once.
But, go now to my brother
And leave my ancient hand to
   bleed —

One Nightmare's End

Dark minds walk with their eyes hidden
    strange creatures sing distantly
    in the savage mountain forest
      (Just spirits of the wind)
    I ask my question silently
    for otherwise my thoughts would hear.
    I am tired, said the painted bird,
      resting in an empty moment.
    I am time, said one still shadow,
      not moving a grimace.
And, we are those condemned by your
      entering through these forsaken doors.

Oh! spectrous phantoms be gone!
A yellow mist, sickening to my sight vanishing —
I walk into summer grass sleeping
    in the sunshine air
    fattened on flower wine
    waiting peacefully there —
I sleep as the dog beneath the painful
    magic sun.

Prayer's Peace

Spiralling upwards through the spinning images
Of the summer town
With soft ensorcelling voices directing
The flow of the dream.
Falling down through flashing levels
    of intricate pain
Towards the hell's iridescent core
Pray now or be forever damned
I pray and am released!

Betrayal

   Wounded skies
Someone crushing
Massive butterflies
   in my hand
And naming
His love hell
The gourd of impurity
   left behind.
My friend once
Considered it justice
And I considered
   it mine
Only to arrive on a fool's
   condemned highway
Crucified in a
Bosch-like jail

There you are
Floating in the wake
Mutated with
   sacks of grief
A madman thinks
And cries out —
And thinks that
I'm his priest!
I ran in terror
   down the halls
Until my sickness ceased!
(My ocean shall no longer be polluted
With the spells of my own madman's doubt!)

I hid from them
   in the darkness
     while the walls
       closed in on me!

I walked with the poison
   in my brain
Stumbling in the
   frozen streets
Hiding from my
Imagination's twisted ghosts!

Freedom's Shout

The world's prison walls break like
Jericho from the shout of strangled silence
Right before the song of freedom
   flashed out of the head by
Shafts of laughter floating like ravens
   perched on a gallows
Where I waited for Summer
   to find me —
Swinging and swinging just for a moment
Right after they released the trap
   and set me free!

Erebus*

After many a struggle and many a tear
I learned their ways which plagued me
   for many a year
I have no knowledge left to use in the maze
   of blood and illusion
Where the people I meet are creations
   of my mental delusion
There is no mirror here which shows my true face
As I stumble down halls without any grace —

I made a living sacrifice of myself the other day
The one love I had, was planning on going away.
   People rushed to my bed
And soon stopped the red bleeding
   and cradled my head
I looked into their eyes and saw they were dead.

I seek a redemption I do not deserve
As my days lost in limbo do idly swerve
With a hidden black river towards the dawn
   of my awakening.
(A genie woman spiralling like smoke out
   of my forehead
Pours highways out of her mouth
O how I long to fly into the land of
   her emerald cat eye!)

How I long to travel the highways that
   repeated unfold
Above my head on a lavender cloud!
People call my name, saying again and again
   What a fool I have been!
Today I lie collapsed in hell
Tomorrow I shall find myself almost well
Travelling these roads not knowing why —

*River of Hell

Ballad

I've got bats in my belfry,
fire in my hair
Sometimes it makes me wonder
if there's somebody there?
Sometimes it makes me wonder
when there's fire in the air.

Been down to the swamps of voodoo
Been to the castles of Hell
Can you hear me in the church
Like some demon ringing a bell?

Saw my baby dying, saw
My heart lying, sometimes
It makes me wonder if
Anybody cares, sometimes it
Makes me wonder if there's
Someone there?

I've got bats in my belfry
fire in my hair
Sometimes it makes me wonder
When there's magic in the air. —

Empathy

I felt the wind blow through me
I was the wind
I felt the stars hold me
I was the stars
I felt the earth pull me
I was the earth.

Prayer for Release

Oh Saviour!
Open the door!
Dread echoes!
Salvage a sick sanity!
As heretics writhe and burn, I turn
My image outside in, inside out
My mind is a heated cauldron
Overturned for You
Like a plague wind I carry all pains
   all charlatan games
A faint martyr and a weary Nature's priest
   my head rolls through the lower heavens
What a strange, bare space!
   and the end of the long race!
Oh drive me
Into Your desert, Lord!

Rainbow-Riding Fools

    Who in the hell are these rainbow-riding fools,
who are so keen at pretending they have found
you when they have not the slightest idea of
where to look for any child of night belonging
to some lost tribe of love's imagination?
    Which group of people are you expanding
      with your hearts?
    I can see just as plainly as you bloody fools,
      if not further, even with my eyes closed!
    Some prophets stand within the breaking of
      each heart,
    It's not easy this hurt that is with me when-
      ever I try to love, try to understand.
    Every time I find someone I use them to
      chase the blues away,
    The line from a song gently heard.

    My heart doesn't break any more,
It just gets down on the ground after dancing
    madly in its freedom, and crawls to a
    hollow place in some fantasy forest and cries
    silently, yet loud enough for all the animals to
      hear,
    I wish I could flow with the river and flow
    like quicksilver easily over each stone or
    debris that blocks my way;
But my prayers fly right and left and
    fall to shatter in their brilliant
    colours, hastily scattering the birds.
      Then I truly know I am alone —

Metamorphosis

With calculation
The insecure fantasy
Blossoms into the delusion
I am growing
In one instance smaller and smaller
Until the blackness of the universe
Encloses my fragmentary illusion
   of martyrdom completely.

In another moment
I am a giant
Breaking free, crashing
Through the ceiling which
Can no longer contain me
I rise to the sky and float
In a mind's time home!

And then a match lit
Burns in the darkness and
Illuminates my futile
Yet sacred reverie —
My mind takes a shadowy form
With hastened flight, vampire in purpose
Seeks to question a new prisoner's essence

The match extinguishes itself
And automatically I awake
Clutching my knees with head bowed,
Facing the bleak enclosure
As glowing electricity of fears
Run like time through my fingers
I might as well be a bird!

Lost and Found

Can't look any further 'cause
I'm the lost and found
Will someone please pull me
up off the ground?

Ones You Drive Insane and Then Say You Have Healed Them!

My madness has fulfilled
my purposes
Yet you have not been astute enough
To respect, understand or interpret
   it in any way.
Essentially, you have polluted it, fought it
You have taken from me
   step by step the lives and
   gifts of those I love —
You build dams for the rivers of
   my growth!
And yet, you fool yourselves and
   console yourselves into believing that
You can seduce me into giving you
   the most precious thing I own.
   My soul

What fools you are!
Already the stake has been pulled
   from my heart
   my fangs are sharpened and I **hiss**
When I think of the blood
   you have drained from my kind
   since the day of creation
Know this — I love the innocent!

This Time

Slow down for awhile
For a good while
Until you find a place to smile.
   (Hard faces are all around me,
   I guess I can't blame them for
   hating me, I've been taking off
   and hurting myself, and now I'm
   alone and have to start all
   over again)
Oh well, I'm not going to fill their dreams,
With cries and screams
This time, I'm going to make it.

Dandelion Wine

How summer's enchantment vanished
   as spring clocks melting began life again,
   fading distant from the golden season, over
   which fired horizons beyond the dark
   mountains call —
I do not know, and perhaps will never know
   for I have been waiting far too long
I turn the flowers' nectar into wine
   to support some dying passion away
   from the love of a cold damp grave,
   a tired yawning earth —
The longing from this magic wine will
Only be to dream a dream of tomorrow or
   to be cast fatefully into yesterday's warm
   rain
   the memories of confusion, love and pain.
For now I am the king of the lost and unknown
   having left my kingdom of seashells and bone
I long to be away searching the emerald
   jungles of imagination for my vanishing
   race!

False Dusk

Roll away mists,
That of the false dusk
Of night, which keep
My childhood obscured.
The different rooms now
Protected against aging.
Doom foretold by
Smoking in the woods,
Where I have seen
Men walking where
Men could not have been.
Where have my fellows gone?
Where have they visited?
While I wandered off alone
Into the rainbow sky?
I swore I would fly
Ships with youths bound
For Minos, who hurry into
Everchanging horizons
Ready to greet their death.
When shall I greet mine?
The voice of rage
And the voice of terror
Are almost the same —

First Christmas Away From Home

The lunatic rose in the evening
He looked to the south
   and scorned the skeleton.
He grasped the hearts of his family
   and cursed them from the bottom
   of his grave.
Soon it would be Christmas
   and he cried at the curse
   so soon sent!
So he turned it into a stone,
   and placed it in his pocket,
     And hung the skeleton on a tree.

Tomorrow

It's not tomorrow that is changing
Tomorrow still rests heavily and
   oppressively on yesterday
God! these ticking mind minutes
   will slowly and monotonously build
   my casket or try
     Written is my epitaph;
The ocean roars over memories
   of life
Spent by its side wondering
   what it is like to die, while winds
   throw dust over dust over desolation.
Is it somewhere else I've discovered
   only to suddenly realize how much?

Stream of Consciousness

I see the flying eagle
With stars upon his back
I hear the iron prisoner
Greet the boy with vagrant lack
I hunger for the hypnotic eyes
And not the vacant look!
I wish to give Lord Jesus
All the things we took.
You mark my book with slander
And words of razor blade
Dame, lady, witch or lover
I forgot your ways —
I've seen the starlit mountains
Where I shall go be blessed
And fall upon a secret worship
Where I can take my rest.
Within a lightning nightmare
I see the setting sun
As faces sear my longing
For things I could have done!
When you were right
   And I was lost
I couldn't stand the longing.
Now dreams beseech the morning
Days with clues of fear and warning!
I wonder where I belong
Now that my war has ended —
Where women weep for hearts
They had befriended
Men hate from fears
And wonder at the dark and guilty preacher!
I raise up my sorry head
Cursed by the cruel creature.

The cards float by
I hear the sighs of all the children
The hermits light, the devil's chain
And worship atavistic
Of the spring time tree —
The summer rain
Have to be done
Over and over again
The nursery rhymes
The heroes' crimes
The villains in the city's games —
St. Augustine, a pilgrim?
Barabbas penitent?
I wonder where our lives were spent
In pettiness and dreaming
Searching in the fields
Never seeing
Never speaking or believing
In what we feel
Touching only once or twice
At things that once were real!
What a gain,
What a cost,
The tears we shed,
The living dead,
The heart as cold as steel
What ghastly ways
To spend my days
In soft anticipation
A silent hush
A deathly chill
An exile's weary child-like ill,
A searching occupation.

Dress Rehearsal Rag: A Ballad

4 o'clock in the afternoon and I didn't
   feel like very much —
I said to myself where are you, golden boy,
Where's your golden touch?
I thought you knew where all the elephants
   lie down
I thought you were the crown prince of all
   the Wheels in Ivory town.
Hey, take a look at your body now
There's nothing left to save
And a bitter voice in the mirror cries
Hey, prince, you need a shave
     And, yes, it's come to this,
       it's come to this,
     And wasn't it a long way down?
     Wasn't it a strange way down?

Don't drink from that cup, it's all caked
   and cracked around the rim!
Well, what did you expect from the kind of
   places you've been living in?
I thought you were a racing man, hah!
   but you couldn't take the pace!
That's a funeral in the mirror,
And it's stopping at your face,
     And, yes, it's come to this
       it's come to this.
     And wasn't it a long way down?
     Wasn't it a strange way down?

Once there was a path and a girl with
   chestnut hair
And you spent the summer picking all the
   berries that grew there,
And you climbed a starlit mountain and
   sang about the view

And everywhere you wandered, love went
  along with you.
That's a hard one to remember, yes it
  makes you clench your fist
And the views stand out like highways
  all along your wrist
    And, yes, it's come to this
      it's come to this,
    And wasn't it a long way down?
    Wasn't it a strange way down?

Cover up your face
There now, you're Santa Claus,
And you've got a gift for anyone
Who will give you their applause —
You can still find a job, go out and talk
  to a friend.
On the back of every magazine, there are
  those coupons you can send
Why don't you join the Rosicrucians?
They'll give you back your hope,
But you've used up all your coupons
  except the one that seems
To be written on your wrist,
Along with several thousand dreams!
    And, yes, it's come to this,
      it's come to this,
    And wasn't it a long way down?
    And wasn't it a strange way down?

Now Santa Claus comes over
That's a razor in his mitt, —
    He puts on his dark glasses
    He shows you where to hit
      Then the cameras pan
        the stunt man standing in —
      For a Dress Rehearsal Rag.

Cheshire Cat

The Cheshire cat sneers down at me from my wall
His smile is so wide,
So very snide,
He makes me want to run down the hall and hide,
But when I return the smile's hanging in the air
Saying "There you are, that's where you're at,"
    I say to the smile "I really couldn't care"
    But I hate everything, especially,
      this winter's gloom
    So I just lie shivering
      Alone in my room
    Waiting for this cat to disappear
      as it smiles fanatically
      and fills me with fear
And he says, "Such is the life, that's where you're at"
    Have you ever seen a Cheshire cat?

Prayer

Lord, see what my twisted
    wilderness has done to me!
Let me rest beside Thee,
    another thief,
Free, in a final agony,
from all grief!

Reaching Out

Running naked searching through the clouds
   just to find the moon
Webs of love stretched from me drawn tight
to the stars, reaching out to remember
   the feelings
How it felt to me when midnight was lit
   within me
Pulling aside dark paisley branches
Stepping into breathless clearing
Calling upon gentle spirits of the forest
I stand naked in the organic dark
Every nerve in my body alert to the
   Soul of the earth
I wait for anything childlike or wondrous!

REFLECTIONS

Reflections

Several old strangers
Mysteriously appear in a
Misty looking glass
   of a troubled past
And strange days of misuse.
One slight hand of error
To fill the transparent moment
   with sudden terror.

The Wall

Gone are sweet days
of forests and carefree ways
Magic memories, your cat-eyed plays —
The woodsman lingers, staring at the oak
While love, like mist, vanishes in fire
   and smoke.
Childlike spirits dance and sway
While I burn with longing for another way
Destitute, aimless, devoid of hope!
White walls, corridors of lonely halls
Greet the angels of the night
To carry my heart
Like a beggar to the light
A witching hour of scarlet dawn, as you
Take my shaking hand to bring me to the
   Edges of dreams,
Passing coldly it seems,
Fading into the land of memories
Where the fools gather without a care!
Where I take to the sky before I fall
   and die,
Across the bridge, He waits for you there,
And beckons silently for us to take
   a chance
Before the morrow and join the dance
Or, forever longing for life in our private
   romance of travel and mystery
Where all roads leave us with all the
   passion and song
Before we rise to fall fast and waste
   away in
The dimensions of our private hells
   and unspoken history. —

We utter a forgotten Psalm and look
   aside —
Devoid of space, devoid of pride
To our world of death and sorcery
Believing in games, where no one
   is free!
Behind walls and chains without
   a key!

The Dark Ways of Instinct

Vicarious vultures watch
And laugh as the hysterical boy
Rushes towards the gates of freedom
Struggling to free himself from the land of doom
The schizophrenic
Often finds the dark
Ways of instinct
And follows his inner
Paths to his own
Personal sun.
When intuition is,
The force of the dog
Finding his master
Then dies in the snow —
There is a trail
Within us when
We were born
The soul is full
Yet empty
Regain the trails
Of love, the
Natural source
Prevails to lead
Us all home
And the smile
Or kiss, may
Disarm the killer!

Magic

The time of the dance returns
   and I go with the flow
   of the magician's magic
I can now say that I believe
   in the world of my experiences.

What meanings do we give
   to the world swimming before our eyes?
We are animal souls tasting
   the nectar of the rose,
The hands of our minds bleed real blood
Grasping at the essence of time's God.

Philosophy

You really recall all the
   catfish catches
When you're living your life
   in the briar patches!

Resurrection

Suffering phoenix flying into the
   past tense of remembrance
Soft flames mixed with the scourge
   of poisoned blood in my veins
Staggering blindly through hallways
   with charred corpses of dreams
Heaven, getting there sometime soon
Rising, Lazarus, out of my tomb.

Spring

The thousand petaled flower of love
   burns golden —
As winter gently recedes
   like some frozen sea
Leaving behind the holy shores of rebirth —
I look longingly as life
   spreads love
As swiftly as the flight
   of the fire-winged hawk —

Thought

Look ahead
The storm
of pain and hunger
freeing itself
discharging
its lightning
and thunder
has lightened
its load

The storm
in its swirl
is a small
yet potent
god of this world
raining over
the mountain
leaving as softly
as it came.

Dream

We wandered
Desolate through
The ancient castles
While reptiles sunning
Disappeared under stones
By waterfalls running
Off the cliff's edge
Where highways ended.

We gazed down upon
The mysterious land
And, in accordance to plan,
Grasped the magic swords
And jewelled talisman
The elfin god had lent
And spoke the words.

There we stood and
In an instant of a
Lightning flash we rode
Our steeds into another world
Where doves sang their song!
I awoke alone without you, my friend —
I awoke away from home
On the mountains of the moon.

Lost Child

        Wise child,
      Child of the end,
      Child of the Seasons,
      Child of the Beginning,
        Child of Christ,
He crosses the divide of night
Crawls through the tunnel of Satan's dreams
To enter the land, dark land of desperation
    He travels down the wild mountain
    And enters the void of insanity
Out of the asylum onto the road of no return
    He becomes the child
        Of lost ways —

Now

Walk away, then still yourself
   when the sea settles
   and the soft air calms
   the ending day.
The sun envelops you in
   its orange tropical shyness.

Flee the Sorcery!

Where the magus leaves the web of confusion
The poor lady reels beneath the delusion
Of greek symbols and delirious odysseys
    A black rose in the air
    The breeze in our hair
    All the day silver —

In the city of hatred, of confessions misread
The dead grasp love from the living
The living from the dead
    All the day silver
    The sun in our hair
    When summer is fading
    With hardly a care —

You, who seek soft asylum, beware
Beware the children of poison, the bandits and priests
Make way for the Lord of the living — leave the deceased
The forsaken rebel, the discordant charm
Seek for the Lady, before a new child is born
    All the day silver
    From the new sky
    All the day silver
Where the swallows swoop and dive in the kindred wind.

Facing Darkness

He faces the darkness
Which exposes his most
Safely guarded thoughts,
Weaknesses, preversities
To the vicious
Predators of the soul
He faces the end as
A naked, unarmed
Man would face the
New world or the
Jungle of passion

He waits gleefully
For the end —
For the death of death
He awakes
And it is over —
Strange within the dark orbs'
Center,
Becomes tomorrow's prophecies?

Dream Journey

The fear of dreams
is like the tunnel
of return
dark and hollow
We step out
into space
and having seen
We leave this place
far behind
to journey further back
into our mind.

A Sad Utopia

Half a city of insane children
Rebuild a sad utopia within my mind
    What is time's whisper?
Red rivers of confusion begin with chaos
As my child-like images gaze at the sky
Sensing wind spirits and clouds going by
We float through the seasons
    Going where?

Retrospect

While you think
Of someone you've never known
    and a person never home
The breeze in the sufferer's hair
Speaks out in hardness,
When its wind is spent
And climate changed.

Precious gold confusion
Grows and springs
    forth in newness
Making each breeze
    softer in the night.

Now I have seen the seeker reflected
Plainly in standards condemned
Aged in tears never felt
    and never shed.
My own image peers from miles away
    and years long dead.
From the lands of semi-created karma
I distantly sweep with my pen
    and make a crude X.

We seemingly venture forth like children
Into what we seek in non- and conformity
A game in which I seek meaning and
    find only non-identity,
  flowing perpetually upstream.

I look forward and cannot see.
Tomorrow we may all grope for nothing.
But as time approaches like
    hunters' footsteps
The ocean sweeps sand away
  and changes a world.

Night

Night sinks
>deep into the stream
>of azure blue
>sweeping past the
>World in a lazy
>>flow.

>Where do days go
When there's time'
>to do anything
Where do they go
When time passes
>so quickly?
Very far
>Very far I know
Very far —

>Where do my
Thoughts go?
Often they appear
>across the vision
Of my life like dreams
Or suddenly
>leap into me like
>half-baked poems
>in the ovens of my mind.
Again, they come as
>silently as the same
>sad song creeps upon
>the sound producing
>machine, and I
>stop and say
>>Beautiful,
>>Beautiful.

Listen

I smile during the swfit invading sequence
    of souls into my room
A power structure of your scientific religions
    of fear and guilt
Makes fools of your worshipping millions —
Isn't it about time you let your prodigal son
    return home?
Or shall you always be trying to convince
Us of the wrong we do?
Tell me, world, what's best for you?
Tell me, who really belongs to the
    salt of the earth?
Prophets of songs, sung in desperation?
Each song a prayer of Love?
Displaced in time among the mundane spaces
Which surround my places.
Listen to the songs before you, in a different age,
    become set apart,
From the culture and message of songs.

Searching

Can't blame a man for trying
It's hard to set a course in a storm
Find a port safe and warm
All the time is flying!
Good girl, I'm crying!

I Have Said Nothing

However I shall see
you across the way
    Your words are wise
    but they have passed
    Your words are good
    but even they have
    passed
    Your eyes are young
    and they shall stay
    Your voice I hear
    in silence
    Your soul said
    nothing
    But I have felt it.

I have said nothing
But perhaps it is
    only what is obscured
    in my words that
    has meaning
Then sometimes meaning
is a dream so vivid;
    so to dwell in our
    heads for such
    instances, until we cast
    ourselves down to believe
"I, I, I, I,"!
    I is there
    and remains unsettled
    like the ocean.
"I" — and then, perhaps,
    another meandering tide
    are waiting for the calm.

It is nothing
    (It's the calling of
    a bird and
the flight of pelicans
laughing at the water)

Listen, Good Fellow Cockrobin

The life on the mountain
Where all saints are told
Grows opaque and childish
With idols of gold
And, good fellow Cockrobin
The souls have been sold!

Freezing

Cold is my touch, freezing
Summoned by name
I am the overseer
Over you.

Fell with nine angels
From a far better place
Fallen from grace,
   fallen.

I'm only breathing,
The flies on my ceiling
Are quietly sleeping,
   sleeping.

I'd thank everybody for
Making me welcome
I'd stay, but my wings
Have just dropped off.

Thoughts

I hear the wind and smell the sea
   far, far away, and I whistle my tunes alone.
Way down the street there is that old house
   and the hasty luxury of it all,
I remember the neighborhood and the
   sight of unruffled birds
   the beach and its remote dialogue
The towering sun overhead . . .
   . . . and now it's cold coffee at three o'clock
   in the morning,
   and listening to old records.

I So Miss Nature's Beauties!

Observing freedom, I find
  a soft burning jealousy.
Receiving the omen of the birds
  nature's close world at hand.
The audacious boldness
  of the hidden man is
Startled by discoveries minute
  and the elation of the
  summer breeze!
  The cadence of invisible forces!
Playing in the forest trees,
  witnessing the triumph
  of the virgin beauty
  in a microcosm beyond me
Fills my soul with stinging dream
  and longing.

I pick up my heart
  up from the midland earth —
And ask the gods of my courage
  for more —
For in the romantic journey
  there exists an obscure tragedy.
In my mind, I follow the horizons
Moving onward with my pilgrimage
  to turn the page of symmetry
    And reach the woman sea —

Rain

Rain, Rain, Rain, Rain
I wish thunder and lightning
I wish it would rain
I'm going to hide in your mind
You'll never know

Rain, Rain, Rain
   Rain, Rain
Goddamnit pour, pour!

Rain, Rain, please rain,
And let me stand in it
Wild and clean and free!

Autumn's End

Burnt leaves fall condemned
  by an invisible dying fire
Stirring in the elusive rotation
    of Autumn's universe.
Our loving child-like ghosts
Run laughing naked
  in the fading Indian summer magic
As if all we shared was a passing verse
    from a Summer song.
Created by an essence which entered unheeded
  from a land of soft sleep,
Created selfishly by a blind magician.
    And I sought glory —
    And closed myself —
  And to the warm sea of life —
  And my madness overcame me
  Like a red fever sent by furies
    from a Druid's hill.
The voices of my dead world
Cried out in the road to haunt me
And I was ashamed and exposed
    in the Winter of my lies.

Ode To the Full Moon

   Thou silver lady of unrest
Thou who decides the action of the seas
Thou who changes the bodies of women
     Who sears the minds of men
     With fever and with dreams.

   I walk the shrouded country
With longing, searching the intimate horizons
To find your temple of mystical oracles
     My double essence is a mixture
     Of awe and of fright
     I view thy resplendent body in heavenly
     Union with land of azure light.

Thy radiance in union with our desire
Traced by the five fingers of my hand
Thy enchanted hand bejewelled in gold and silver
     Summons my confused soul
     To walk into waves until I am no more
     As if beckoned by the sirens of ancient lore

        Thy cold embrace of light
        Giving birth to all
        Dark silent creatures of night
        From the lover's sorrow and plight
        You, like a jealous goddess, steal delight.
        Yet, sweetly give thy blessings
        To the youth and maiden who have
        Set their vows on the path of right.

Dolphin

Dolphin, child of Atlantis,
   she rode upon me in an
      ancient sea.
Soon I became a man but once
      on land,
I longed for the sea!

The Sea Child

    As every day grows weaker
And the summer grants me no passionate reward
    For the war of winter
Each immaculate tiny castle caustically melts
    Beneath the absolute heat,
      of the many repetitious mantras.
Stranded, atrophied, upon a desert shore
    Like a dolphin drawn by
A magical obscure genetic remembrance
    The sea child dared to leave the sea!

The Man of War

Now I can see it
it disappeared
a purply, blue and amber stone
inhabits it.
I approached it and reached out
to touch it,
but it quivered
and when I saw the tentacles
I abandoned my mission!

The Vision

Down in the
Center of the
Myriad world maze
He travels in
Shamanic trance
Of nameless possession
He wanders in apprehension
And longing for each new hallucination,
And each new Apocalyptic vision,
Which bring him further and further
From this time and into all realms
Of fiery fear and rebirth
As he gives voice and names
To the unknowable and unnameable entities
Which enter his mind and dreams,
To part with their existence
Lost in his dreams as he tosses,
In confusion in sleep, tortured by the vision
Of universal death.

Reveries

Idyllic scenes, the passing of seasons
    across the untouchable vision
    symbolic of the pentagram of release
    framed by prison windows —
The feverish consciousness delights
    in reveries of the unattainable —
Watching birds in pairs, build their nests
    which, in my hopes are blessed.
The racing energy which burns my sleep
    expands my mind
Leaving my body, tiny helpless and blind —

Pulse is quickened by the devil in
    the season of love
Silver shafts of light
    through the shattered night
Break free from the moon shine,
To close my eyes and pass in a moment
    through walls of eyes
    in dark disguise
To travel down the stairs to the door —
Swimming in the phantom lake
    soft lady of my fantasy
Water child diving into the pool
    in the heart of the wood.
        That's it —

Walking the streets at home that's fun
    like an acquitted murderer.
The animal heart beating wild
Knocks upon the door like a Biblical child —
I know what I want to do now —
    I want to walk by the sea

The circular world of ocean - sea
    in the womb of darkness
Enclosed, as if in a crystal ball.
I see myself watching the birds,
    the sea birds,
Circle so freely over head.
With melancholy thoughts I rest my head
    against this creative shore
I witness the death of the future
    within the universe —
    within my imagined sky
        The vision fades
          the seabirds cry
            at the end of it all —
              I open my eyes
                with a sigh —
                and
                    that's it. —

The Long Ride

Nightmares rode me
Nightmares rode me
  My life long —
    long
Oh, please forgive me!
I meant no harm.

Advice

The only duty of man that is
   worthwhile developing is the
capacity of living within his soul.
Hell is the incapacity to do so,
   either living or dead. So, folks,
   respect yourselves.